Rodin's Shadow

Patricia McCarthy

clutag / AGENDA EDITIONS

First published in 2012 by

Clutag Press
PO BOX 154
Thame
OX9 3RQ

and

Agenda Editions
The Wheelwrights
Fletching Street
Mayfield
East Sussex
TN20 6TL

Design and production by JAC design
Crowborough, East Sussex

Printed and bound in Great Britain by
TJ International Ltd, Padstow, Cornwall

Patricia McCarthy is half Irish and half English. She went to Trinity College, Dublin, after which she lived in Washington D.C., Paris, Dacca, Bangladesh, Kathmandu, Nepal and Mexico. She has lived for many years now in rural East Sussex where she was Head of English at a girls' school. This is her second full-length collection. *A Second Skin* came out from Peterloo Poets in 1985. Another collection, *Around the Mulberry Bush: Selected Poems* is to be published by Waterloo Press. Her work has been widely anthologised.

In memory of my dearest friend, Annie Mooney, who found for me, in an open-air second-hand bookstall in Westport, Co. Mayo where she lived for many years, a book in French on Camille Claudel – which inspired this whole sequence.

Acknowledgements

Thanks to the editors of the following in which some of these poems have appeared: *Acumen, Agenda* (William Cookson), *The Irish Times, Irish Press* (New Irish Writing), *Scintilla, The Warwick Review, The London Magazine, Poetry Salzburg Review, Molossus World Portfolio (Sudeep Sen)* and *Long Poem Magazine.*

A group of these poems was read in a dramatic performance for two voices in front of Rodin's 'The Kiss' in Lewes, Sussex in 1999, and, in a performance for five voices, in The Turner Contemporary Gallery, Margate in July, 2012.

A special thank you to W. S. Milne, Tim Liardet and to Andrew McNeillie for their huge support and encouragement.

Cast

Camille Claudel, 1864-1943:

Mistress of Rodin and talented sculptor. Sister of diplomat and playwright Paul Claudel. Rodin said that she was more talented than himself. When Rodin refused to marry her, even though he had promised to do so, she had a brief affair with Debussy. She then became more and more depressed, thought Rodin was persecuting her, and ended up being carried out of her filthy flat on the Quai Bourbon in Paris, and taken to a lunatic asylum. She was moved to the asylum of Montdevergues, near Avignon where she was locked away for twenty eight and a half years. She never sculpted again. Her mother was very unsympathetic, cut Camille off, and for many years ensured that she could neither send letters nor receive them. Her brother, Paul Claudel, kept away from Camille for years, afraid, it seems, of the similarities in their natures. It is suggested that there was something incestuous between them when they were growing up. He labelled her life a terrible failure, but finally felt very guilty that he had neglected her.

Gwen John, 1876-1939:

Mistress of Rodin and talented artist sister of Augustus John. Born in Pembrokeshire but lived a long part of her life in Paris where she befriended Maud Gonne. Her obsession with Rodin was similar to Camille's. Where Camille had been brought up a Catholic but lost her faith, taking refuge in 'madness' when her affair with Rodin ended, Gwen took to God on the rebound from Rodin, and became a Catholic in c. 1913. Both women died anonymously. Any references to Shakespeare represent Rodin's insistence that both Gwen, and Camille, read Shakespeare to him in English and in French.

Rose Beuret, 1844-1917:

Semi-literate long-standing companion/partner of Rodin. He married her purely to preserve his art works in 1917, the year in which they both died.

Claude Debussy, 1862-1918:

Composer whose works mark the transition from neo romantic to modernist periods. Known now mainly for his piano pieces. He wrote 'La Mer' in Eastbourne where it seems he had a clandestine affair with Camille. Despite other women in his life, he was broken-hearted when Camille abruptly broke up with him. He kept Camille Claudel's sculpture, *The Waltz*, on the lid of his piano until the day he died.

Clara Westhoff, 1878-1954:

Sculptor and neglected wife of the poet, Rainer Maria Rilke. The latter was, for a time, Rodin's secretary.

Auguste Rodin, 1840-1917:

Famous sculptor, known as the progenitor of modern sculpture, although quite a traditionalist himself. His works are housed in the Musée Rodin in Paris, where Camille Claudel has a tiny room dedicated to her work.

Contents

Front cover: 'The Other Island', oil on canvas 102 x 81 by Bruce Killeen. Bruce Killeen lived for a long while on the Isle of Mull with his wife who founded the Inniemore School of Painting. His work has been exhibited widely, including at the Royal Academy, London. He has lectured in Art Schools and was, for some years, Art Correspondent for *The Guardian*. He now lives in the Gers region of South West France.

'Camille, allez viens! Viens vers la lumière!'…
'D'autres chercheront, d'autres écriront, d'autres'…

Anne Delbée

'You make your life
Let it be consciously, with fearlessness.'
        Gwen John: A draft jotting to herself, headed 'Thought'
        (Sue Roe: *Gwen John – A Life*)

'La sculpture comme les autres arts se retire dans cette chambre
solitaire où le poète abrite ses rêves interdits. Camille Claudel
est le premier ouvrier de cette sculpture intérieure'…

Paul Claudel

'Le grand point est d'être ému, d'aimer, d'espérer, de frémir, de vivre.'

Auguste Rodin

Prologue

Song Stitchers

Tutored by Penelope, we stitch our songs
together, gathering echoes of footsteps lost
to masters of stone and script as we trip along.

To each thimble's flash, the work shapes up
without us, words threading themselves into texts
of hearts absolute, whole, wanting only to cup

the great simplicities. Penelope examines the songs
we sew into their music, edges ragged from ages
of troubadour and cave, torn too long

by lightning's needles. While language unpicks
itself into its silent origin, she unravels
more strands for us to tack onto pages thick

as time, thinner than onion papers of missals.
In a dumb ventriloquy, we bind patterns and themes.
Penelope holds up a finger blistered in complicity.

Waltz with me

The Waltz

La Valse, bronze 1895

*The posture of the great Angel (at Chartres) is not so
very far removed from a dance movement.*
                                        Rodin

    (pianissimo)

Waltz with me; blend with me.
Don't tread on my heart.
Hold the stars in my bodice.
Its astrological chart
needs no teller or crystal
to say that I might fall
if you unsteady me now
in this dizzy secret ball.

    (poco a poco al forte)

Sway with me; fancy me
in taffeta, silk and lace.
Press your thoughts through me
as, like a genius, you trace
my filigree, my jewels,
my crescendos that swell
into contrapuntal threnodies
for the truest steps to excel.

    (fortissimo)

Partner me always
in triples of time
until, as one great Angel,
we swing through new rhymes.
In your arms as if forever
I glide by your side.
Oh waltz and waltz through me
who should have been your bride.

Take me

Take me to the mountains
that you might fold the heather
into tracks for luck. I shall darn,
with pine needles, the holes
cut in us by reality and create
new stitches for the seconds shared.

Take me there, that your dream self –
which I know now much better
than you – might slink away
and I can shake your hand.
There will be no need
to touch. Your very presence

will caress me intimately.
Stand me against a larch
that I might stretch without moving
into the heights you cause.
Take me to the mountains –
just once so that the rocks

and gorse might camouflage us
against those who, elsewhere,
would judge and gibe. The wind
will rinse out our accustomed lives.
Only too soon the eagle will swoop,
the mountains move away.

The Gossamer

Camille Claudel: *L'Abandon,* bronze 1905

The girlhoods I have lived and could have lived
in Villeneuve, Paris, I shall give to you,
have you the talent to shape me, the touch to play me

while we waltz backwards, formally at first,
under the rope of time, then more intimately,
through trust, gaining spot prizes for our affinity.

Over the sprung floors of your youth, you can dance me
into the small hours until we are composed of light,
twirling gracefully into a truth that would never invite

such precarious balancings upon wires strung tight –
between the exhilaration and despair of our present plight –
over horror stories, shock headlines and cruel blights.

Can you hold the gypsy soul in me, we will take flight
on bare feet, stamping, into the castanets of our hearts,
wild tarantellas that, colouring our blood, depart

from those ballroom steps which old masters would impart.
Instead of those girls from bygone parts,
I will be the gossamer webbing our two hearts.

Hotel Room

Rodin: *L'Éternel Printemps,* bronze 1884

Anywhere: the wooden bed we lay on
to the turning of a key, over ghosts
of light and shade, polish and dust.

Flickering candles etched me for him
on the papered walls as he flirted with
silhouettes of chambermaids who advanced

and withdrew from corners of his lust.
Did I not satisfy him, I cried –
as I metamorphosed into his Eternal Spring,

his muse. I changed in and out of onyx
and jade, letting him claim me as a trophy
beneath all my skins as he liquefied me.

How far we flowed into one another...
Like the highest tides bursting gantry,
dam and groyne, we spattered with wrack

the gilt mirrors. And reduced even the sea
to a governable, inland force, framed now
by his body which contained my entirety.

Opening the window to reverse, with iron will,
the owl's path; I stuffed the dark
into my pillowcase to prolong such gracing.

Then I slid behind his eyes to a room
with a different number lest, powdering
my face in morning's smeared glass, I would be

too shy to stop day's menial tasks: shapes
replaced by lines, locks picked, pillowcases
turned inside out, laundered again.

Broken Appointment

In the long slant of this autumn day
I await you, defying legends of loss.
I wish to share my mortality, frail
as a leaf, with yours and unmake the hay –
taking different harvests in as we shed
glories not related to decay off our skins.

In the long slant of this autumn day
I sit vigilant, unsure which special traits
of yours to store, hibernating already in you
while the sun sweeps the lawn with its rays.
But morning mists threaten the new angles
you haunt, darkening the light in my wrists.

In the long slant of this autumn day
only our provisions have not been made,
nor our patterns crossed with rusty shade.
Unable to sleep or wake, I pick from the clay
colours of war and flame, burdened
by the interplay with your absent name.

Cleansing

Do not wash me off before you go from me –
with water cold as an empurpled winter sea.

The speedy splashings I would rather not hear
while I am erased – lest she might peer

too closely at your pores for signs of infidelity.
Like a Veronica-cloth I require your skin to be –

printed indelibly inside and out with my hues.
Between the soap and towel do not undervalue

my need for your fidelity to me; for my lipstick
to remain upon your cheek; for where I kiss, lick

and melt into you to be preserved as telltale signs
of a Midas touch. Too harsh a scrub would define

only the guilt which I want kept from me.
Wear me boldly, advertising me all over your body.

Let me hear no drip from a tap, detect in the basin
no sud to insult the water-falling tides of our union.

Camille Alone

Femme Accroupie, bronze 1885

While I weep, alone in my blacked-out room,
you are being fêted: your long-standing woman
at your side, toasting each other in Chablis.

I see her name scrawled over the plaster:
Rose, Rose… Each heavy vowel, a perfume
distilled by habit, sticks to your clothes

long after it has gone. Its luminous label
you cannot disown. Against my four walls
I have pinioned you, you claim, by trying

to force from your fingertips, if not
from your blood, the one affirmative
which would enable us to be together.

Behind chandelier-lit windows I crouch,
listening to shared jokes, to comments tossed
convivial around the table. In its polish

you might, for a second, see me mirrored
before the cutlery, silver-plated, crosses me out.
I hide here in the different light of our affinity –

which needs no ignition but flickers
secretly in your eyes, despite your words.
In my hands, I hold our intimate expressions

and touches, our useless passion injected
in what I sculpt. While, in mannered homage,
you kiss the cheeks of all the invited ladies,

I chip away at myself, paring skin down to bone,
dried rose petals and drunken laughs on my breath.
I order myself to be marble, flint, uncaring stone.

Rodin's Shadow

Is it because our tides rise uncontrollably
above their watermarks that, for control,

you place the dark side of the moon under
my armpits which perspire with your sweat

and steal for your mask her grimacing face?
Do you require me to cast your shadow

in nights consisting only of that shadow?
Then, in days shortened for winter, that I drape

my body over its own lengths which drag
like a train imprinted with knaves cutting strings

of marionettes? Despite the trees flagellating,
with their own sticks, the back of the wind

in full view of saints and sadists,
we struck up so much light together –

I thought we could disown the dark.
But keys turn in the pores of your skin

and weights hang from your aura
fashioned by angels from webs, wings

and filigree threads. While you push the earth
over on its belly, I am so close to you

that I reflect your blackness, moving
away when red scratches crisscross your back

from my doing and steel clamps hover over
love songs which abate with an eldritch screech.

Dissolving your shadow upon my tongue,
I mount the moon again in a star-crazed sky;

place my bewilderment on the ebb and flow
that resumes with an underarm hair between us.

Sea Change

Sorcerers place on your head their hats.
Fitted into each other, their pyramid
rises as I squat in the upturned point

of the one in your hand. Your draped lids
hide your eyes which change from marbles
to fish-like slits and back, erasing me

so that lust can float in the garbles
and smacks of a glaucous tide meant to spawn
lace-lines of poetry. While frayed ropes

coil around you and metal helmets, torn
from divers' heads, encase your own, cutting
off your senses, I hear the sailing ship

meant for us strike against wrecks jutting
from currents which throw up their own bedrock.
And I know a momentous sea-change has happened:

pebbles wrapped in weed flung against rocks
like dice painted by waves not in our favour.
Little point in juggling with the hats –

for the gulls, my white mystics, take cover
on shaky feet, their wings left behind
to hang, snagged, from driftwood. As the salt

created from our sweat drains back into my mind,
the sorcerers laugh. How did I ever think
that, between us, we could drown the ocean?

Indian Summer

Journey in Touraine with Rodin, 1887

We have made the terms: to keep a hair
between us and stretch the shadows
of shortened days. Yet it is our heat

maddens bitches, injecting vermilion
and sap into the sultry scapes imposed.
Brittle leaves grab us like hands

needed for holding at once each curve
and pore, but we grind them upon
the dopey paths of flies, fixing suns

into which our hearts have burst above
rowanberries the rainmakers count
that spot hedges with blood. Wordless,

our bodies rave over one another,
the primeval light from our eyes
rising with pastures where beasts lope,

invisible, trying to swallow all fire.
As you point across the caged vines
to a tanglewood famed for black masses,

we are not certain what it is obsesses us.
And pray that the keeper of the bell
might allow from the old clock tower

a few halcyon hours still, beating
against the distance a time foreign
to calendars and dials which will not

force us back through dark, but permit
dives into mirages from steaming wires.
While hazel-nuts ping on fiddlers' bows

and apples outgrow sin – with a desire
whole enough to be love while it dares,
we know there can be no tempering.

A soft knocking

Could have been a miscarriage...

A soft knocking in my pulse alerted every cell
so I swallowed your reasons like nutrients
and stashed you in arteries as I quickened
into soil in preparation for your festival.

I closed my eyes to hares and rocked you
in my pride, glad my body, gifted with continuity,
could be more than a hunter's relief map, its hills
and valleys greening into playgrounds long due.

Now you've gone who never came despite poultices
of bitumen and brimstone. Without thinking of you
I hear your heart drum in songs that make flesh
other than yours and translate into my silences

your fable. Still fending off groping hands,
I pretend you've been kidnapped, that I'll sweat you
from my pores as the sea does the sun,
trapped into parturition by morning over land.

What good: each search-party's interrogation,
my poverties and droughts for ransom?
My blood flows north of limbo, not of my kind,
a killer's, confirming your obliteration.

The Rodin Sculptures

I have sculpted and sculpted you
from unknown quarries with axe, chisel,

> scissors, mallet – studying you
> as you sat: torso, limbs, head

from every angle. I have placed
my heart inside you; felt you,

> fathomed, lived and practised you.
> I have offered you up to watchers

who, with notebooks and rulers, copy
your cool assertions of plane,

> shadow, curve, framed by your ethic
> for work nonstop. You have let me

trace your remotest thoughts,
hold you in the gravity invented

> by our chemistry. I have inserted my hand
> between the stone and its unfingered interior.

I have counted your pounding pulse
when you broke out of your contours –

> beyond marble, copper and bronze,
> outside inspiration, dedication and craft –

to exist with me in every context.
I have sent away the watchers, removed

> stepladders, varnishes, plinths, let the air
> mould you into enhancer, diviner, magician,

maker – dependent upon me
because unable to come to life without me.

> So many maquettes, not yours, not mine –
> flesh upon stone, unquarried, are we.

Actions, not Words

Nothing more to be said.
From under my carefully made single bed,
I am pulling out the woman I was for you.
Wrapped in layer upon layer of clothes
bought with frivolous abandon just to impress,
she flops like a rag doll, stuffing gone:
heart-spent, dry-mouthed, come to this.

Nothing more to be said.
No point in buffing her cheeks brick-red
with some exclusive pomade, in massaging her
back into days echoing you so loudly they burst
the phantom eardrums of birds, when you turn her
on a maypole round and around, bewildering
firm bearings, ransacking the familiar.

Nothing more to be said.
Too long has she been postponed and misled
by non-committal moods of suns and storms.
Too trustingly did she offer hard-won wings
to ease you from the entrapment of old tethers
into a music no string, reed nor stave had known,
challenging the points of every star.

Nothing more to be said.
The clandestine is outworn. Strip the beds.
Only your actions, now, could salvage feathers
and flowers to court her with, piercing the impasse
in which you may as well take her for dead.
Hand in hand with last chances, she and I bend over
backwards for a deed to prove your constancy instead.

Rodin's Model

*To Rodin, a model was more than a means whereby the artist expresses a
sentiment, thought or experience; it is a correlative inspiration to him. They work
together as a productive force.*
                           Hidden in the Shadow of the Master, Ruth Butler

He plaited my limbs into the stars;
wound them around trees – like ivy.
He stretched my frame between suns

and moons with no apology; turned me
inside out until even my intentions
and thoughts, as if wired, became bendy.

An adventurer of the soul, he tied
in knots my tolerance, watched me put
even my stilled self on hold to excuse him;

do double-jointed moves to accommodate
the cartwheels, handstands, jugglings
in his blood as he veered from *love like hate*

adore kiss court marry – then back –
magnifying and mortifying me. How
to survive the sudden holocaust of feelings

that hang me upside-down, torn apart –
now that something has snapped, finally,
in my over-pliable sucker of a heart.

Camille's Bust of Rodin

bronze 1888

I sculpted him from my skin,
then tapped him into bronze, his profile noble

from every angle. Flattered, he called it
definitive: my bust of him, and hoodwinked
experts it was a self-portrait on his plinth.

I skipped around him, buffing
his cheekbones with my palm, streaking his beard
with chestnut lights from my waist-length hair.

There he swanked, his face naked as the nudes
in a live frieze around him, my gaze on him
a mixture, still, of intoxicants and rewards.

In turn, I offered my own head, for him
to study like a phrenologist until it emerged
from an unworked block of stone. So much his,

I could have sworn it would stay forever in his hands.
Yet as usual he withdrew, defining as pressure
my need of him. My Rodin head –

a stranger's now, tarnished, ghoulish green –
I mount dream-high on plinths of a premature elegy.

Letters Unsent

Camille Claudel: *Femme lisant une lettre*, bronze 1897

i

From the Château d'Islette, near Azay, 1890 where Camille
was sent by Rodin to recover from a possible abortion

In the record heat meant to be ours,
I have been seen as a woman flying
out of a window with a red umbrella
to set fire to forests which cannot

burn out. Holocausts of sunflowers
are mourning, in black bonnets,
their own martyrdoms, attesting
to a sun that crackles as it sets

all day, red, over your absence.
You would only have had to be
in my midst to embrace me. Unlike
the sky which needs to study

its own image in water in order to
court the charred land, we would need
no reflection. We could have made up
beds of rivers never before stripped,

have composed on the mesh
of mossed tidemarks a new gush of music
for our lineage, giving – to receive
in the river's tempo our own currents.

Yet the crime of our pact to deny life
by your not being here cannot be
covered up by the greenest slime.
Too much time has elapsed and no time

for me to give each singed sunflower,
each smoking tree, my dream of you
on which to thrive. Without you, I am
a pyromaniac, at the bottom of each ravine.

I fly back in through the window
with the red umbrella, pacing up and down
as I count the hearts I have torn from stones.
I let them cry out to you.

From the Château at Azay-le-Rideau where Camille
was staying alone – to Rodin

I cannot write to you.
Stylish sentences tear from me
ghostwritten to swank confidently
as impostors in a foreign tongue.
Posing to their best advantage
they shun the guidance of my hand,
forbidding me a cue.
Worse than all the drafts
of silence is their final copy.

I cannot write to you.
Your skin should be the notepaper,
my fingers the words. The unwritten
alone is meant to be read and you
are looking over my shoulder, author
of my world's night-long dawns.
Only to the unsent do you
regularly reply. Your express mail
my mind to itself delivers.

iii

From the Château d'Islette where Camille went alone

If it could, my body would speak to you
of its own fields surveyed by the woman
inside myself – who trusses the tinders
of range and vale for the passion,

still, of a high fire. Not resigned
to weeds growing up makeshift fences,
to parched rivers losing their sources
in lunar months forbidden any menses,

she coats stones with gilt to pave
plains shaved by tongues of traitors.
Then claps at the desires disowned by me
which writhe into a cabaret in my craters.

She does not know how, resigned to loss,
like her I dream of you returning
to spread parklands over my geography,
uniting the three of us in one burning.

Abortion

To kill a child, to kill an immortal soul, it is horrible! It is awful! How can you live and breathe with such a crime upon your conscience? Note that a person who is very close to me… has been paying for the same crime in a house for the insane for 26 years.

Letter from Paul Claudel to Marie Romain-Rolland, 1939

Feet up in stirrups I lie,
a strange jockey mounted
on distress, counting the minutes
racing to your rejection.

Although the going is good,
I fall at every fence,
my smile at the doctor a way
of weeping over the jackpot

for which I can't compete
but, kept, would have had
to be given away. I wish
he wouldn't banter like that.

I'm not his accomplice.
This morning started wrong,
my threshold of pain already
too low to tolerate injustice

to you. I should have donned black
instead of multi-colours,
reverently coping. Courses
unfinished before practised me

little for this. The nurse
hangs on me the weights
of her euphemisms as I wonder
what victory might have been.

A broken bone, I pretend.
With hands stupidly cupped
for you in Moses' baskets,
just as well I can't hear

the rocking horses bolting
from their rainbow-runners
into the grins of bookies
as the final post bends

in two. Crouching low,
still, over your loss,
I land all wrong on the stretcher
where, without substance enough

here even to die,
backstreet courtesies
cover you dark as turf, dark
as the choice I didn't have.

To substitute, regrets shy
onto the pad between my legs,
stakes lost, and I am lonelier
than an empty grandstand.

'L'Age Mûr'

plâtre, circa 1894; bronze ancien, second maquette 1898

She did not have to dream that she was old.
She saw spiders' webs turn grey; the sea
wrinkle, tired of expressing itself
on a surface cut short by horizons.

She was not stale: just that experience
had deflated the peaks over which she leapt
into a darkness unknown before –
when nights fooled around with ghosts

and bats hung like leaves from arms.
Easy with a body crayoned in by dreams
to lie low, young, in fallen birds' nests,
cold-shouldering the day's hard lessons –

insisting to Methuselah that, because
in her prime, she could dispense with day
and light for the hours she walked
her own inspiration's path, sufficient

to make forests outgrow their height,
the sources of her thought inventing
rivers without bank and bed that ran off
every map, uncontained by oceans.

No point in tears for what was lost
on altered levels, for things never named;
or in attempting to fit what came about
into mythologies older, more strange than hers.

Overnight it seemed, she wheezed out
her pension of air: a second child stooping
for canes to splint each fractured bone.
She did not have to dream that she was old.

Unborn Children

Camille pétrit la matière pour enfanter ses créatures à elle.
Ce sera sa seule maternité.

Reine-Marie Paris, *Camille's grand-niece*

Little Girl with Doves: painting 1898
La Petite d'Islette: marble 1895
La Petite Châtelaine: Natte courbe, bronze posthume 1893
                 Natte droite, bronze posthume 1895

Dancing in a ring around the limbo of my thought,
these fairy children, fading as I examine them,
plait my dreams into a skipping rope,

and play 'pass the parcel' with my sorrows,
layer by layer unwrapping the void, their gift.
I hear them sometimes chanting sweetly

their chosen names: Agnès, Emily, Hélène, Hortense,
as they rummage around my womb, all girls,
shaking coloured rattles of their own seeds.

One lies in my canvas still-born on a beach –
mourned by doves fanning her with white wings.
Another, whose head only has appeared,

lies breached in bronze. 'Maman,' chorus the rest.
'Breathe us at least into the air.' Which is what
I do. La petite d'Islette stares up at me

from her plinth, asking for what I cannot give.
Her sibling, La Petite Châtelaine, sits for me
day after day, hour by hour – plaits pinned up,

plaits down – showing me her longest faces
full of wide-eyed pain and anxiety for the only life
I can offer her: petrified forever in stone.

Dancing in a ring around the limbo of my thought,
the fairy children turn their backs on me.
Their skipping rhymes fade into elegies.

False voyages

The Sea in his Eyes

In Eastbourne with Debussy

As a long-ago child I competed to be
    the first to behold the spangled sea –
illumined by the sun into an ancient script
    of make-believe legends by which to be gripped.

Then I saw it in his lived-in eyes –
    imprinted with charts and the bluest of skies,
imploring me, a mermaid, to sit astride his tides,
    drop wings, not anchors, from my sequined sides.

The fathoms held keels and fins and wrecks
    of fleets on horizons which appeared as specks,
conquests and losses etched on shells,
    unscrolling from a beard, my old Neptune's spells.

While the waves scribbled their indelible scores
    on cliffs that crumbled behind yellow gorse,
the Seven Sisters looked up, looked down
    chalking us into ghosts from the town.

I wished to stay in that sea, miles away
    from a cross-channel sludge-green turned grey.
As it meditated on histories, I heard you say
    we were children, still, in the tell of its sway.

The Sweetened Fiddles

Debussy speaks

The motes of light I touched you with –
as if you were composed of all the elements –

 shimmered into chromatic scales. Up, down,
 my rapid fingers riffled the tides,

dedicating to you their arabesques. Yet
on Eastbourne promenade, you remained

in a sea-haze, artist of silence. You petrified
my notation in the chalk-white cliffs,

dismantling horizons I'd turned into staves,
gagging black gulls. The arpeggios

performed by water slapped against wharves
copied themselves in my secret manuscripts

while I followed you like a score, adding trills,
crush-notes to treble and bass. Despite your claim

to dislike music, you gave me the naked flesh
of ultimate sound to compose into courtship

in the small hours, diatonic systems disrupted,
clashing keys. For your daylights

I conjured harps whose glissandos slipped
in folds off the backs of waves along

the percussive shingle. Shocked at my need
for a sudden eternity, I tried to practise finales

at tea-dances with you under chandeliers
in the Grand Hotel. But the fiddles, strung

with your nerves, sweetened their range,
bows alive, as if it had just begun.

By the Sea with Debussy

Camille Claudel: *Beside the Sea,* marble
Rodin: *By the Sea,* plaster 1906-7

Did the keel-less boats jangle shanties of warning
and alarm to you as I stared out into the blank open sea?
Or were the clanks of anchors dropped by jetties

a comfort when we tripped over stunned fish,
driftwood horizons and amputated wings of gulls?
Making out sails in your heart's high-running tide

that threatened to dash my defences, I left your side
for the lea, and strode, with pebbles for eyes
and granite limbs, along a road like a sailor's rope

looping and coiling the maddened sea.
How should I have reacted to the wind whistling
the music of your voice and body to me when the boats

in the inlet seemed painted with hope, jangling
a far-off unforgettable chant, singsonging, songsinging
about false voyages sinking in self-made quicksands?

L'Artiste du Silence

Debussy to Camille

The terrible hush
of snow falling
is the hush of you gone.

The steps are white
piano notes stuck
in C Major, no sharps
or flats to be worked upon.

The terrible hush
of snow falling
is the hush of my soul

which lost its virginity
in meeting yours
and, without a touch from
our bodies, became whole.

The terrible hush
of snow falling
is the hush of you gone.

White manuscripts
for claw, foot, paw and hoof
bind themselves into annuals
for unsung orisons.

Lace Letters

Camille in the Isle of Wight
to Rodin, 1888, after repudiating Debussy

I wanted to send you lace letters
trailing in wakes of the finest ships

which vanish before forming yet leave
a certainty that they contain
exactly what you wish to receive.

I wanted them to darn rifts, frill crests
wisdoms of their art woven into a water

rippling with treasure from wrecks
and caves, with patterns from currents
that have touched bedrock.

I wanted to send the longest lace letter
of the entire ocean, not just its seams

or edges; to let it swell into a mastery
of waves fretted with knots the envy
of sailors you tied too soon in me.

I wanted to untie them in the roughest surge
against a wharf – knots so complex
they became simple reminders of you.

I wanted to send you lace warm
from my body, antique cream and new.

I wanted to send its hesitant motifs:
wintry branches against the sky,
gulls' bleached wings against the black.

I wanted to send you lace letters
you could neither receive nor send back –

I wanted to send you my own samplers
to replace what would not scoop up;
to have, in the choppy wake of qualms,

more than only my writing looping itself
into lace on the page's dead calm.

Shed wings

A Silent Valediction

from the Pyrénées where Camille Claudel was taken by Rodin,
and another time by Paul, her brother, addressed to Rodin

Go, go into the morning, deaf to drums.
There are crows enough to send you off
and clouds to leave behind faint bruises.

Sweep through mists, shaving your face
on mountain edges. Know that – for you –
this woman would have slapped her life

against a wall to dry into kindling
and offered up her lengths of hair. Go –
regret not the valley's floral show,

its rainbows. Laugh off intensities
in new clearings, borrowing the armour
of rocks usually her dice when heights

penetrate you with music. There's work
for the asking beyond those mountains
which stand like noblemen, shirking contests,

backs turned on your courses. Go.
Leave her washing herds of wild horses
with songs that would only make you poor –

before her river grows into a sea
and she words you into tallstories.
Consider simply the ravines at your feet:

never a heart's dichotomies. Go.
Chosen before the sun, you cannot backtrack.
Perish, with her, from reality.

To Rainer Maria Rilke upon his Rodin Book 1902

No mention Rodin made of me
when describing his measured walks
with Rose in morning's virginal hours

where he noted wild animal and tree
standing in their own propriety.

No whisper of our greening bowers
in winter's depths. Of how he entered
my every cell to produce planes
and hollows of such primordial power

that you defined him as Nature,
not man, ruthless in selection.
No hint as to how he excavated

whole civilisations in a sculpture,
my womanshape teased from curvatures

in mountain ranges of celebration
in his marble's perpetual moonlight.
No nod at the molten metal I became,
warm while I flowed; at his elation

as I solidified in his hand, snatched
from my own space. Or did he claim
his work a theft from a mythological past,

the anonymous silent stone mindless
of my weptover songs never despatched?

Tell me he owned up to just one thought
of me while he crossed with her
of a morning over my shadow on every path;
how he balked imperceptibly at my lack.

The Louvred Shutter

Tapez contre la persienne, je vous parlerai mais je ne pourrai pas vous ouvrir …
                                                        Camille Claudel

If, by chance, you pass by,
tap against the *persienne*.
I shall not be able to let you in

but I shall imbibe your presence
through the slats, keeping you,
for safety, as a smudged taboo

rather than as a definition.
I shall whisper an acknowledgement
like a breeze through the grille

but offer no word, wary of stirring
that maze of levels and layers
which spirals without path,

post, exit or explanation –
to the tightest box-hedged centre.
You must stand as if for ever

on the outside, accompanied
by a rustle of dresses and chatter,
footsteps and horns that would shatter

the dark in which I am immersed,
sleeping completely naked
in make-belief that you are here.

You will not see my soul you rebuffed
hiding in a corner in hand-knotted lace,
nor my thickened waist which needs

your arm to cinch it in. Pause a moment –
that I might cease imputing to you
a mercenary's pacing. Then continue

on your way beyond old hopes and dreams
which tap with woodworm against the *persienne*,
insistent you are no longer my man of men.

Your Hand

Auguste Rodin: *La Cathédrale,* stone 1908
Camille Claudel: *La Main,* bronze, vers 1885

All I want is for you to leave me your hand:
its warmth to enclose mine, its protection
to stay me under a roof in the worst of weathers;
its passion to match mine, fearless in intensity;
its way of talking in squeezes to enrapture me.

All I want is for you to leave me your hand:
left or right, it matters not which – to change
its pattern of withdrawal – until it gives,
totally, cradling my hand in upsets and in dreams,
in the reassurance nothing is what merely seems.

All I want is for you to leave me your hand:
its flexibility to cope with the brutal, honest words
I give it, at times to cup; one of your fingers
to inscribe 'I love you' on my palm's fateline;
the conversion of your heartline into mine.

All I want is for you to leave me your hand –
its cathedral within which to worship – that my hand
will become again the one you sculpt into grace.
Under Islamic rule, I want to chop off your hand;
to keep it fisted in my soul even if unmanned.

Persecution

Je suis au bout des forces.
                    Camille Claudel 1905

From 19, Quai Bourbon

She barricaded the doors, insulted
the concierge in the courtyard,
her voice high-pitched, changed.

On thresholds, she laid mantraps
and tripwires to stop him burgling
her ideas and dreams. The advised tisanes:

burdock, plantain, she drank to be cleansed
of the poison injected into her veins
by his abstention. Yet the rats he placed

in her mind jumped from sewers
over her lonely shoulders into the light
dimmed day-long by closed shutters.

King rats, queens, jokers – all staged
a pavane for the feral cats inside. Shrouding
her coarsened body in a long velvet coat,

grey and motheaten, she brandished
a broom-head of nails and like a tramp
patrolled the night. Her shadow,

dressed up in pain as for some festivity,
grovelled for pickings from every gutter –
jeered back at her from the Seine

whose silks had once encircled her waist.
Onto cobbled quays whose bridges
concealed clandestine lovers,

she spat her abuse: *Bâtard, monstre,*
gredin, beast, canaille, torturer, fouine, thief...
Skin thickened, she trudged along.

With nails dipped in bottle after bottle
of vin ordinaire that she swigged,
she scrawled in red on walls: *Rodin Rogue,*

Rodin Huguenot... Old humming songs –
emptied of his voice, touch and passing charm –
rolled up with thin fags in her bed.

Exercises for Two Hands

Every morning you might hear them
from the Quai Bourbon: the thumps

on rented walls as I make dextrous again
my hands calloused by clay and cracked

from stretching too far over his heart,
the limited filled with reckless infinities.

I start to work in dawns: hiding-places
re-opened in the winded breath of statues.

Lining up rickety props of scaffolding
from abandoned studios, I balance

on shed wings, convincing myself
that severance is inseparable from meeting.

With masks of ancient stone boundaries
about me once more, I settle in shadows

of outsiders in crowded galleries with all
we did and did not create in flesh and stone.

You will not guess what season it is
when my soft, beseeching hands hold

the vaults of that secret cathedral sculpted
by him from them without any posing;

when I interview the space held
instead of me in his well-known arms.

Massacre

*Un monceau de plâtras s'accumule au milieu de mon atelier, c'est
un veritable sacrifice humain.*
                    Camille Claudel

Preparing for the unburiable act of burial
at the back of her blackest mirrors,
she takes out axe, mallet and lines up

her sculptures which stare her out, claiming
to be part of her which, as part of him,
exists no longer. Prepared for the sacrifice

and without emotion, she steadily thwacks.
Profile, limb, torso. No blood is let.
The percussive blows accompany dances

of nerve-endings on the spot. Even chips
and jagged defacements have the power,
still, to pain and to resist the flames

of the stubborn passion against which
she warms her toes. Last cries of accidental souls
quickened in her works by the sweep of him

revive the torchlight, limelight, midnights
when he prowled around her with an artist's aim.
Like a spectator, staring herself out, now,

she cancels the carter hired to inter the remains.
Leaving behind no address, her key
under the doormat, she goes off to piece together,

in her head, the ashes she has made, full
of ghosts of failed promises and old spells.
No one will see her in strange cities digging up

paving stones indented by anonymous feet –
to be carried home upon her back counter-signed
and ingrown. No one will listen to the women

bent on her acclaim, untethering ages from stone.

Requiescat in Pace

I am painting your name in loud colours
on the gravestones in every churchyard in Paris,
outraged at having to practise death like this –

with no requiem except the unaccompanied silence
of each moment without you; no saining ritual,
myself the sole mourner, a black band

constricting my heart. Were it not so messy:
our Love in the heads of flowers unfastening
from memorials on the right and left bank,

I would order plumed ebony horses and a carriage
to transport the emptiness, my life dragging down
the remains of time, its cortège without a wake.

As it is, I reject the hands of those angels
meant to guard me, and ignore the ghosts
of the grandest couple we could have been

who wander into distances down boulevards,
through parks, creaking gravel paths. Only
the screech-owl holds my pain in its midnight cry.

The Seine knows I still know you in my bones
as it slinks along, holding in its span the mirage
I was for you. Devils dance in its currents,

laughing at the years that have come and gone
and will come and go without us, while scaffolders
pull you off the points of steeples and stars.

In case of regrets, you might find a vestige of me
pressed between the parchment of musty hymnals,
or in the tuning whistle for Gregorian chant

where I forbid muffled vespers from aisles to hint
that you were not worthy. Requiescat in pace.
Candles flicker at the desecration of my offertory.

Letter from Camille to Jessie Lipscomb
from the mental hospital

Dear Jessie,
>   I have been taken away
>   to this grey house of Bedlam.
>   I am meant to walk upon my head
>
>   or sit, petrified to stone:
>   exactly what he wanted.
>   My name, once magnified
>
>   in the same breath as his,
>   has been buried in the number
>   by which I am newly christened.
>
>   Sedated by futility,
>   I have no passion to sculpt
>   or draw – except caricatures
>
>   which punch and cackle
>   in my slapdash lines. From mouth
>   to mouth I catch jumblings
>
>   of unedited stories, inserting
>   puns and jingles as I rival
>   the other inmates in games
>
>   of compulsive delirium.
>   If you came to visit,
>   you would find no touchstone
>
>   in me, though I am less locked up
>   by their bunches of metal keys
>   than in myself when I wept
>
>   at my own lack of compromise
>   and cut him off. Circumspect
>   by practice, I subject to scrutiny
>
>   these completed works of flesh
>   staring me out, made
>   I think, by Rodin in disguise.

House of fools

Crown of Thorns

On my head now: the spiky crown
        of a mad queen
in a kingdom of tight-lipped gaolers
        who have stamped out
courtiers, diatribes the only homages
        in the chamber of this has-been.

An expert with mallet and chisel,
        I nail myself to the person
I was whose life, unfinished, I slipped.
        There – on the Isle of Wight –
she is for a break, hosted by waves in the sea,
        sculpting her own season

from cuckoo flowers, wood anemones
        and primroses on lush banks.
She laughs through lanes of her woman-world
        into the yellow trumpets
of daffodils that blare out a fanfare,
        offering the sky thanks

for their brief existence. Here – resignation
        hammers me onto the back
of the chair on which, stiffened, I sit out Time,
        hands inert on my lap, confusion
no more than that riot of remembered colour
        on verges, a thunder crack

despite clinical labels. As keys turn in locks,
        I summon her: the former me,
as my only visitor, along with the light
        which lets itself in to the cold
every dawn. Handing me a whiff of the spring
        she once shaped, she watches me

plaiting and re-plaiting those wild-flower stems,
        weaving them into my crown,
fingers septic from splinters. While she tries
        to plant invisible bulbs
in the stone floor of my mind, I shift a little.
        I cannot be taken down

from any cross, yet the thieves – of my reputation,
                   of my talent, life and sanity –
she hangs beside me on black gibbets of trees, on
                   cursed crucifixes of winging crows.
The damp rags she puts to my face to preserve it
                   as some posthumous effigy

new-cast are no Veronica-cloths. She cannot
                   save me from misjudgement as I die
alive, dumb songs on my lips: hey nonny,
                   hey nonny, hey nonny no – no touch,
no man, no woman, no thought in my nunnery
                   of white skin, my crown awry: Ophelia's.

Take me back to Villeneuve

Je voudrais bien être au coin de la cheminée de Villeneuve, mais hélas! …
Letter from Camille to Paul, her brother, 4 April, 1932

Ce joli Villeneuve qui n'a rien de pareil sur la terre.
Letter from Camille to Paul Claudel, 3 March, 1927

Take me back to Villeneuve
to see what patterns the ivy
has grown upon the walls,
feel the sun on its mellow stone.
Here icicles hang from my window
like daggers cutting me in two.
Le Mistral catcalls through cracks,
making the poplars in its path
grovel, with me, on the ground.

Take me back to Villeneuve.
This prison no one deserves.

Take me back to Villeneuve
to witness the swallows nesting
still in my childhood eaves;
to hear the sane screams of swifts
between roofs; never again
the cacophony of the interned.
I dream of sitting by the open fire,
perfumed by its applewood –
at peace again *chez moi.*

Take me back to Villeneuve.
This endless sentence I cannot serve.

Take me back to Villeneuve
to be hidden away in its cellar,
not this concentration camp.
Triste surprise pour une artiste.
I push aside the varnish
and clay they give me for my métier,
my chosen freedom: to do
nothing but write letters
they censor, count the days –

Take me back to Villeneuve –
and make lists for tea, wine, preserves…

Take me back to Villeneuve.
Fly me out on my iron bed
in my charity clothes.
I'll have an eiderdown at last: of sky.
First class, third, fourth class –
all classes sink into a single calvary
in the cells of Montdevergues.
Swap my number 2307
for my Christian name, Camille…

Take me back to Villeneuve.
It was only a crisis of nerves.

Camille to her Mother, Louise Athenaise

La sculpture est le besoin de toucher.
                    Paul Claudel

                    i

Mother of my first light –
was it your luminous shadow blowing up the night?

Why were bee-stings couched in your lullabies,
as you christened me with words you had to confess

then swung me in linen, bleached and starched,
between bedposts of narrow boundaries?

Mother of my first cry –
did you fill my eyes with tears from your sky

so your formal outline would settle in a blur
as you pushed me out from under your skin

like a débutante in salons and polite côteries?
Did you want my curtseys to flatter and to defer?

Mother of my first rejection –
was it your long-accepted family tradition

to blind and gag girl children – then to stand
before me with no lap, smile or rocking arm:

the first ever stone I could not sculpt
which pushed me into a métier you banned?

Mother of your own shame –
was I not to be given a life with the name

you chose for me from a book of flowers?
Did you dress always in black in mourning

for the daughter you would have liked me to be:
cut from a pattern, with no mercurial powers?

Mother of your own severity –
in your shipshape world, was it your economy

you wished to hand me down with your sewing box?
Did you not see, in my darning, I chiselled the holes

slashed in me by your tight lips into the nudity
feared beneath your bourgeois smocks?

Mother of your last gasp
and my first breath, why did you disown, not clasp

to your breast my living death; be proud of me
despite the bough I felled on your family tree?

ii

I could have swapped, for intensity, the thoughts
cancelled by your maniacal chores, have lit candles to stir –

mother of my abandonment –
your warmth. I could have taught you to consent

to caresses – with my need to touch and touch.
Mother of mine, apron-sharer, watch me now remove,

from your bun, the pins stabbing the silent decades
without you. Feel, still, how I clutch.

Stations of my Cross

(According to Paul)

Aprés une vie extrêmement douleureuse, elle a abouti à un échec complet.
                                                    Paul Claudel

> *I adore you O*
> *Paul my brother*
> *And I praise you because by my cross thou*
> *Hast saved thy*
> *Privileged, well-*
> *Travelled world.*

With the saw of my tongue
sharpened on Rodin,
I cut it myself from all the trees
killed off by depression
in the asylum grounds.

Eyes in walls watch me,
pelting sightless stone visions
at me as I walk its way.
Each step blots out the mystery
of a love better directed

at God. Too weighty, the cross
digs into my back, pushes me
down on all fours. I stop
countless times in the intersection
of timelessness with incarnate time.

> *I adore you O*
> *Paul my brother*
> *And I praise you. Because I was your*
> *Warning mirror in which thou studied*
> *Thyself, thou*
> *Hast redeemed*
> *Thy world –*

not the world I am consigned to,
condemned to a wasteland within
and without by a Pontius Pilate
in drag whose edicts deprive me
of all assistance, all letters

from external unwalled worlds.
And the case I plead for myself
falls deaf on the ears of assassins.
Smiles in family photos far-off
twitch and jeer at the green wood

which bows, sags and warps
old blessings upon me, swinging
through their consciences
where I remain half-pietà,
its knots twisting about my heart.

Too long have I carried a cross
planed by a false god;
too long watched it mimed
in miniature in flying shapes
of midges, mosquitoes, crows;

too long beheld its dark outlines
thickening the iron grille
and staining the window
behind which I sit, imprisoned
in my determination to show

no emotion throwing off
every day's lengthening shadow.
Despite constant surveillance –
my hammer salvaged
from a Parisian atelier with R –

> *I adore you O*
> *Paul my brother.*
> *Know that hanging myself, beyond pain,*
> *On my cross, wormeaten, rickety now,*
> *Has become my*
> *Sole redemption.*

She hears of Rodin's death

She read the obituary notice in the paper
and sat on, legs apart, motionless, her hands

warmed in the deep folds of her colourless skirt.
She stared out of the window at the sky.

She did not register in her notebook the skein
of wild geese flying across in the formation

of a wave, rustling like taffeta from the ballgown
she had worn with him, clapping their wings

in intimation of something far off. She read
the newsprint again until it squiggled

into lines of ants queuing up for take off
into her mouth, her eyes, all over her body,

forcing her to be a black effigy of bereavement.
She felt nothing. Nothing except relief he was

out of reach at last. No one could have him now.
She resumed her scribbled lists: *cherries*

in brandy, coffee, sugar, flour, ticking off the day
like any other on her home-made calendar

to mark the blank time. As the geese swished back
through the sky they had cleared, wings creaking

like the oars feathered by Odysseus in his escape
from the sirens, she sat on. She would fashion

a new ballgown from her crêped skin, then
dance in it alone: slow, slow, quick quick, slow,

so slow she would stop moving, desired forever,
the dance of love a stasis in death's strong arms.

Mistress of Rags

The Voice of Rose Beuret

Mignon: Head of Rose Beuret, an early work by Rodin, bronze circa 1869

Mignon, mignon,
                mignon –
mon pétale, ma fleur,
                ma fleuraison

he called me in the small
                and great hours
of our life-long liaison.

Mignon, mignon,
                mignon –
Loyal he was, he said,
                as the swan

while he sculpted my head
                to the applause
of the city's carillon.

Mignon, mignon,
                mignon –
mon pétale, ma fleur,
                ma fleuraison.

Mistress of Rags

And there were other lessons Rodin wanted Rose to learn, especially how to wrap his clay sculptures with wet rags to keep them from drying and falling to pieces before he could preserve them in a plaster mould. Rose would go on doing this until the end of her life.

Hidden in the Shadow of the Master, Ruth Butler

Rose to Camille in the asylum

Slip slap slop slip. Slip slap slop slip.
Rags in a bucket I squeeze and dip.

From behind your curtain, I re-appear –
his *garçon d'atelier* down the years.

My wet rags I wrap around your face:
blindfolds and gags that can find no trace

of the youth that you once trumped over me,
causing New Year days of mine to be

alone, in tears as he squandered money
and flowers on you. My turn for pity.

Slip slap slop slip. Slip slap slop slip.
I lay upon you my soggy strips.

Like your sculptures, you must not crack.
From the curved ladder of your back,

I remove dry rags that have unrolled
where, fallen to pieces without sanity's mould,

you need shaping again from your own baked earth:
Clotho's flesh in tatters, dying into still-birth.

Poor old maîtresse, Odious C, sad effigy
of the beauty you were: on a par now with me.

Slip slap slop slip. Slip slap slop slip.
These rags I shake, pull, twist and rip

from the curtain behind which I re-appear:
Madame Rodin to you. Have no fear.

No punch-ups this time. His first love, last dust,
I wave, then leave you to the nurses' trust.

Slip slap slop slip. Slip slap slop slip.
Fresh rags of words for you from my lips.

'Cet homme couvert de femmes'

i

Theirs the best of him: the passionate, tender man
whose fire they could feed on, as in the early days
with me, when I wasn't old always, *poor old Rose:*

that silent little washerwoman behind a curtain,
the illiterate servant who loved him until death:

not always the Rose overblown under his breath.

The best of him theirs: precious stolen hours
not demeaned by the daily with his shout
for dinner when it was late, the banishment

to my room when a King came to call. Their bowers,
love-nests, pillow-talk needed no duster or broom

coated by the blackest of his moods with gloom.

Crawling all over him as protégées, equals
they never endured insults like *grumbler, leech,
une sauvage,* never burped from leaning over

to button up his boots too soon after a meal.
Fading with his clothes, how would they exist

at his side, only by the sun ever kissed?

ii

Portrait de Madame Rodin, Mère, circa 1870

Invisible too long, even in the oil painting,
my tightly closed lips and frantic eyes
could not explain the shadow across my face.
I did not know whom I was meant to replace.

Invisible too long, the bust of that girl
windblown, alive, looks intensely from the frame.
She is not Rodin's mother as the label claims.
Broad-brushed, she bears my name.

Watch her emerge at last, forever young,
breathless in her dark velour dress
and white neckerchief, her identity in her hand –
with a story and lifeline upon which to expand.

iii

Playing me down because of the whirlwind
buffeting him over you, Camille, he would not
have confided the highest times of our minds

and hearts when, in the early days, on a diet
of eggs and rats, we walked arm in arm into fields
and forests, wrapped in my womanly light;

when he constructed cathedrals from arched boughs
of spread trees for me, and pressed me
to his heart. How often we re-took our vows

to be 'we' rather than 'he' and 'she'. No share
for you in our treasure-box of memories:
like his desire for a good fairy to pick me up in the air

and take me to him, our dreams of each other, needs
and loyalties stirred into a hotpot for sustenance
in adversity. After you, other rivals tried to succeed.

Their names lisped from his lips in sleep: Gwen,
Claire, Jeanne… Yet you were his queen paramour.
I saw you in his eyes; how depressed he was when

you cooled. I listened for the arias or double breaks
in his voice, told myself there were ways to love
and ways to love – as the loser in all the stakes.

Duchesse

A *Duchesse* I was in the Pavillon Musée,
        his unwanted gift to me.
Left to myself for six years I learnt from my parrot,
        lime-green, mimicry
of the sycophants, his bacchanalia on paper,
        of the sweet-talk to his bevies.
I had other touches than his: Coquette the cow
        licking my hand, the monkey
tame in my arms, the dog jumping onto my lap.
        Ignoring the dignitaries,
I counted on my beads the pheasants, magpies,
        at ease in my own company.
I picked mushrooms for the coachman, apples
        from forbidden trees,
lawn-grass for the horse. Head high, I banished
        every trace of idolatry,
from my country seat, towards the high altar –
        so sacred – of his artistry.

Le Mariage

The Villa des Brillants, January 29, 1917

The jokers ushered us in to where we stood,
side by side, on our last legs, last gasps,
like guests at someone else's wedding.

While I coughed and he tottered, the vows
were pronounced, no deep look, no kiss,
a cheap brass ring half a century late.

I tried to recall his faded love-words: *tout
à toi, O that I could press you to my heart, enfin
mon petit ange.* But I heard only his tired voice

taking its cue to titters as he swore to me fidelity.
I wanted to pull his beard into a train, long,
white, carried behind me by our first passion;

forget the other women I had put up with
for his art's sake. The sighs, expelled
by him into the cold winter air, placed a veil

upon my head. And he gasped Yes, yes, he
would give himself to me for the eternity
of his sculptures, to save them falling, robbed,

into private hands. Yes, for the showcase
of the Hôtel Biron, his Musée. I did not call
witnesses to the thick band of the sunbeam

I had worn for years on my finger,
granting me an accustomed exclusivity
through cracks in ill-fitting window-frames.

Our frail bodies, places of worship no longer,
were ruins of the cathedral arches studied of old
by him – as we struggled up the stairs

to a 'honeymoon' in a double bed for nights
and days, dust our confetti. With no coal, we clung
rigidly to each other, caricatures of lovers,

our hearts shaking with the walls from explosions
in a munitions factory. Jokers dismissed, I could die
in peace, his bride: in extremis but also in truth.

Two thousand letters in two years

In two years, Rodin received close on two thousand letters from Gwen John.
Susan Chitty: *Gwen John*

.

Rebirth

Most of all, Gwen still longed to write poems.
He was more than her master, he was her god.
Susan Chitty: *Gwen John*

Dear seigneur, since meeting you I've written poems
I'd be too embarrassed to show you; my feet
have moved of their own accord from cinders
into glass slippers. I try to be distant, discreet.

Yet people say my face has changed at my eyes
and mouth, my tongue has a new secret pliancy.
In Meudon, St. Cloud or Paris, were we to meet
I'd speak in franglais of things so ordinary –

meanings hidden in funny accents – that you
would wonder if I spoke at all. In my silences
you might hear ice break, resonances of seas
and the present bursting into hot-house tenses.

Should you remark you'd missed me, I'd think
you meant someone else because I am not me –
just your invention, a carnival in my senses.
Despite my shyness, self-deprecation, insecurity

I think perhaps there is some youth still in me.
I can feel again the sun rising daylong in stones.
I keep saying it's not true – nervous of vulnerability –
how I am re-set among flowers in the mountains.

While I slip acrobatically between public sheets of light,
learning that making poems is really making love,
I give your *Thinker* thoughts too deep to question,
slap oils over my poems to the roucooing of a dove.

Letter from Gwen John

87 Rue du Cherche-Midi

Dear Camille,

I am painting you in your asylum room:
its floor abstract, no proper ground
for your feet, its hard, poker-backed chair,
the light only what remains in your eyes.

I am installing you in my wicker chair,
offering you my grey silk blouse, stockings
bought in Bon Marché, a tailored dress
to swap for the shapeless garb you sit in

reflecting inwardness, tired of looking out,
Your composure is what I strive for: collected,
recueillie – mistress of yourself at last.
I am hanging at your grille the glow

of shifting landscapes, composed by my brush,
that will take you back in turn through
the Celtic stretches of Britanny, Broad Haven.
Haverford West. I am collecting for you

all my rooms – their corners, infinite spaces:
the copse where I slept on crackling leaves
in the Luxembourg Jardins, the wallpaper
whose pattern I could never forget, the fire

in the grate and pink parterre of 7 rue Placide;
my attic room here, its ceilings sloping into
angles of mysterious light. I am reducing the chair,
now, to a shadow, yourself to a space to illuminate

your endurance, your lack of expectation –
unlike mine in rooms wherein I wait and wait.
I am painting you in your asylum cell
where we both trample on *his* old calling cards.

The Julie Letters

Camille Claudel: *The Gossips*

*Rodin suggested Gwen should write her letters to an imaginary female
correspondent, 'Julie', and tell her about everyday incidents and events …*
                              Sue Roe: *Gwen John – A Life*

Dutifully I addressed them: to her name –
a manufactured correspondent, a *cocotte,*
causeuse, pretending to be who I am not.

P'tits riens and *bêtises* from café-tabacs
boulangers, pâtisseries, I reported verbatim
in their minutiae to 'Julie' – to amuse him,

my 'tendre amant'. How he lapped them up,
relieved, that, in obeying him – *remerci,*
he was freed at last from my epistles' intensity.

I loathed them: the *histoires* after *histoires*
I reeled off, with a sudden garrulousness:
a bird in my wardrobe, shade of my new dress,

how Blanchette's hair had been curled
in rags *chez la coiffeuse,* the cost, the croissants
delivered too late – *catastrophe* – the silence

in Notre Dame's dark nave when le curé
fell down the pulpit steps. *Mon dieu.* At least
communication with him had not ceased.

How thin it wore: the daily mask, charade
as he dictated my diet, reading, myself at bay –
when I craved, strongly, to have my say.

Levity after levity made him smile, but
a ventriloquist's torture as he shrunk me
to the shadow I was, his virgin-floosie.

My other raw letters I read back to myself,
willing him to catch like fireflies
those blown into backstreet gutters with sighs –

in favour of the snippets I polished and signed
John, Marie, your obedient little model, cocotte.
I should never have become who I was not.

Linguist

I am learning to speak his language again:
chains of lexicons impossible to pronounce.
My body is conjugating his, breath by breath,
the method direct without grindstone or cane.

He is working up me from my feet, ensuring
I enjoy the course. Idioms retained
subconsciously return as I listen, immersed.
From between my breasts I am procuring

manuscripts of old romances. His scents
I have tried to spirit away are overcoming me
once more, my mouth pouting like his, gaining
confidence for the phonetics of daily chants:

He am, I is. My eyes he re-invents
as epithets to explain, not adorn. My brows
specialise in circumflexes, my forehead
is dashed with grave and acute accents.

Touches of words confuse their genders
as he drills me in divers tongues. How can
the present possess so many tenses?
The silence, in its own dialect, tenders

impersonal pronouns and double negatives.
Its wall-charts depict nothing but wall.
Yet, instead of trying to break it down,
I am interpreting fluently the fricatives

of unsaid speech and their many parts
which are parts of him. I am longing to say,
on this crash course, how I understand
his hot, cold and lukewarm hearts

Rose, Rose, Rose

Rose, Rose, Rose – I saw your dignity
in each of the pink paper roses
Rodin gave me, everlasting in my cheminée.

Sewing lessons you could have given me
how to hem invisibly, cut out patterns,
tack, interface, and seam with industry.

With your thimbles on all of my fingers,
I could have re-designed serge uniforms
for endurance, off the backs of malingerers

even if my pins in your pincushions
had lost their heads. You could have helped
choose wild silks, grey and vermilion,

and ostrich feathers for home-made gowns
with false labels from Bon Marché for us
to catwalk in the Hôtel Biron – up, down

over the mosaic of his own black stones.
Both bad spellers, we could have laughed
at malapropisms, misnomers, especially my own

as I jiggle with rules in French. Such comfort
we could have had backstitching,
unpicking from our lives every hurt.

How literate you were in your illiteracy.
As I pull off his pink paper petals,
Rose, Rose, let me honour your dignity.

Cats' Chorus

Camille Claudel: *Le Chat*, bronze 1893

Camille and Gwen

We both knew them: the bat-hung nights
under wool blankets in no one's arms, no sleep,
half the bed's cold sheets, in the courtyards cat fights.

We both arranged them: the starched white pillows
plumped up with old endearments; blue, yellow
and green cushions humped head to toe

in a vertical line beside us like a lover, body-long,
inert as the wardrobe, chair, as the silence
cutting the air with its cruel lack of song.

We both shared them: womb-positions in darks
devoid of dawns; sleep-walks through dreams,
the head-butting of rejection in vacant city parks.

We both owned them: the cats with green eyes
that stared through our cracked, too-giving hearts,
saviours to our confidences with their purred lullabies.

Edgar Quinet, Tiger, blind black *Valentine,*
alley cats, feral cats, strays shadowed our steps
while we assessed ourselves in their coats' sleek shine.

We both made them: camps in acacia bushes, pines,
no soft-talk, no sweet-talk; only stalkers blocking
our view of Rodin's window, and the twisting vines.

Minou, chaton, puss-puss: our frequent calls.
Our own scratches, spits, claw-marks – in self-abuse
and self-protection – we ascribed to caterwauls.

'One of those little stones'

It is blessed to have been, for a moment, one of those little stones.
Maud Gonne: *Servant of The Queen*

Of course Yeats loved her:
her cheekbones jutting out like cliffs for him
to jump from into her heart; her eyes telling
over and over her charged, action-packed story.

I should have painted her,
brush-strokes not stilling her rebellions but
performing them as she resisted any frame.

You could have met her
with me, Camille, in her attic rented in the rue Passy
for storage of dead marches, banners, revolvers,
potatoes grown from seed by her for the troops.

She would have shown you
the leather blinkers polished with saddle soap she wore
to blot out the ghost of herself in a green dress and a lady –

a shadowy, persistent lady
veiled in grey who rang a bell on a piano, indignant
when no longer called up; blinkers to avert her eyes
from packs of cards shuffling of their own accord

while Madame Blavatsky talked.
Starved of love in your asylum years, you could have
added to the numbers of those famine victims.

In white inscriptions she listed them
on flags stitched into squares torn from darknesses,
blacker than the blackest widow's weeds tailored
for her perpetual wear, blacker than the sleekest feathers

of the Morrigu, that great crow-Queen
of battle which she became. She would have offered,
for your blank walls, a seething mural – of the wounded

stitched up by her auburn hairs;
red crosses over upended crofts, their tenants landing,
evicted, in enforced handstands; children famished
into stick figures of chalk scratched on school blackboards.

To her chant: *Fire is the heart of stone,*
we shadow each other over mountains to acceptance,
pushed by obsession into the action under action: of art.

Gwen's Prayer to Rilke after his Death

Gwen John: *Portraits of Mère Poussepin 1915-1920*

Dear Rilke, Rainer Maria, Maria Rainer –
the eight faces of Mère Poussepin are frowning
down at me from the portraits I did of her

on the convent walls. I am turning you
into a false god, she mouths: the first mortal sin
since my conversion, caused by my need to revere.

Forgive me for my past resentment of you
as *Mon Maître's* ghostwriter. I required missives
in his own distinctive hand: red-hot epistles overdue.

I beseech you now, my friend, to grant me pardon
for my hostility at your siding with the Duchesse
de Choiseul who, proffering bananas and bonbons,

discounted my existence as if I were some waif
off the streets entering his studio for dubious reasons.
You thought her one of your workaday angels, no demon.

Yet her so-called earthing of him was caricature
to me when she stumbled around to music-hall medleys,
loud singalong waltzes used for her overtures.

Did you not see a vision whirling in, scarfed in chiffon,
out-performing her with folk dances from the Auvergne
while the phonograph accelerated at such graceful allure?

Rainer Maria, I could not bring myself to recognise
warnings in the *Love Letters of a Portuguese Nun*
you lent to me on purpose, her solitary guise

hard-won. Too obsessed I was – hanging on for him,
sewing past pillow-talk into silken cases, envying cantatas
in alleys of copulating cats – to succeed in all my tries

at self-containment. How hallowed you are:
Rilke, Rainer Maria, Maria Rainer, in star-read skies.
As I travel along your lines to you, my avatar,

I hear Mère Poussepin falling from all her frames.
Backwards, forwards on my beads, I mumble through
worlds cracked from the radiance of your name.

Afterword for Gwen

Had she opened the parcel of clothes,
sent by Ursula Tyrwhitt, her English friend,
the double knots on its string hot-waxed

in red, she might have survived going
to interpret the swapping scripts
on a sidling Channel sea. She could have

unravelled the cashmeres, unpicked
the dresses, corselets, blouses, pulled
the straw from brimmed hats –

re-working the textiles into a life
to be wrapped in, thimbles silvering
the ends of all her fingers, bells

on her toes. She might not then
have submitted herself as if a squiggle
of paint on a palette scraped of colours

to the passage from dark to light
over water, mixing the *cinabré vert*
from finished paintings into a high tide

that demanded epitaphs as she collapsed,
anonymous, in a Dieppe street.
Had she opened the parcel of clothes,

she might at least have been warm
as she ran away like a cat to hide
in the screwed-up face of death,

with no luggage, even, of a self. Prayers
should have been said, her hand clasped
that night in the hospice bed where she lay

like an outcast. Instead – another parcel
was wrapped up, her existence returned
to a fatherland, unframed, of infinity.

'Liebe Clara'

Word-Bells

Clara Westhoff to Rilke

i

Epistles of light etched in the sky in your beautiful hand
from Muzot, Duino: vast insoluble questions waiting to expand

from jottings whose inner life anchored you to things:
Gothic cathedrals, pressed heather, portraits and paintings –

the Louvre, Jardin d'Acclimatation, Jardin des Plantes…
There you waited for secrets of statues, for streets to descant

to you a syntax wherein you would lose and find
yourself. Castles injected their turrets into your mind

until you could swing words like bells, and women, animals
and earth happened to you like events, important only if capable

of transformation into poetry. You didn't mind stunting your life
like an unplayable organ – for you clung to the belief

that what you commented upon was taking place elsewhere,
the nearby distancing itself as if painted on silk in an affair

of colours: pearl-grey houses, rainbows of booksellers' stalls,
brown bindings, green albums matching the green squares, walls

lime-washed with your lines. Stood always as if before
something great, like a painting by Cézanne, its musical score

fixing the vital ground hues, forever removing indecisions,
you invited the sea to impose the sway of its ellipses and elisions

upon whatever in you had become bewildered and confused:
bits of people like brush-strokes the Impressionists used,

the perished animated still, floating in a wind from nowhere,
falling and overtaking each other in a fountain, aware

you were a maker with the roots of centuries in you,
how all the time past, time to come would happen anew.

*Liebe und werte Gräfin, Dear Princess, Dearest Friend, Dear Lou,
Dear Clara, Liebe Gnädigste Frau,* you wrote. *I long to hear from you.*

You must feel your emptiness, you said,
like a vacant room around you, like an arch
through which comes breath warm as bread,

scents and solitariness in bottles,
and autumn appearing in rust, gold and red
like a visitor out of season – to create

the wind, its accomplice, overhead,
piling sky upon rushing sky, decorating
lanes with vertebrae of the leaves it bled.

No mourning for you – your task to use
the joys and splendours of life, your Muse,
while old selves enacted miniature deaths,

and your best selves remained at a remove
from the loved one who could not pass away
possessed without possession
to encounter the infinite, breath by breath.

No mourning: grief for the vanished future
an immeasurable legacy without sutures,
Death not the banished stalker prepared

to pounce, but at home in fields of blossom,
seasoning life. Goethe calling for light,
Beethoven shaking his fist at thunder, like you,
in their final hours refused to be spared.

No mourning: your excuse for absolution
as you passed in, through and away from women
who gave themselves to you, while regularly

you gave them up, sidestepping precipices
of the Love you approached – to perfect it
in that Solitude which preserved you,
you claimed, from petty perils of the daily.

No mourning. No wake, no widows' weeds.
Yet, hand in hand with Death in your elegies
you remain the requiem-maker for our exequies.

iv

How the smallest bird voice
                        hit you and concerned you.
How a bird's nest appeared
                        to you an external womb
furnished and hidden exclusively
                        by the female who trusts
the universe like her own body
                        and sings in it as if singing
in her own inwardness, no distinction
                        between her heart and the world's.

v

What you wanted: long walks barefoot in the woods,
growing a beard day and night, lighting an evening lamp,
a fire flickering onto the ceiling your moods;

the moon to visit when it suited her; to be mobbed
by stars while you translated rain and storms
into gods; the company of books, hog-skin bound,

and of maîtres like Rodin, Jacobsen from whom
you could learn; trimmed box hedges, wild-flower-summers,
bowed rafters from some dark, remembered room

and the familial smell of old wardrobes heaped with things
into which you metamorphosed, given the gift of seeing
with your body, of breathing with the pen, renunciation

identical to fulfilment. And O the saying in every pass
you made at women, their glances blinding as the sun
while they stained themselves into cathedral glass.

Behind your stare, the blood of their colours
filled you with longings, with fantasies of security
which made you live, always, beyond yourself.

Russia, Paris, Vienna, Bremen: journeys
away from your life-sized life that wronged you –
and on to Munich, Pisa, Naples, Paris again, Capri,

never escaping the hinterland of your Self,
your solitude in bad hands, unless in your own.
Places, departed from, turning into bright hours:

of deep sleep in the open, each pavement stone
more familiar than a pillow cut from the slab laid
by Jacob under his head; angels grafting their bones

onto yours, changing the visible into the invisible
and back, excelling human action with velocities
of a higher reality. You, too, surpassed

mankind to look back with overtures
of compassion, radiating your presence, expecting
nothing, rinsed and run clean like Nature.

What you did not want: a worldly home,
an exercise book underlined in red by Life,
to arrive incomplete at the present;

the abyss over which you perched, psychoanalysis,
lost innocence, to be dragged up a mountain of pain,
a heart battered, embittered and formless;

the lighthouse sending out signals beyond you,
not meaning you, not knowing you,
its light a question mark threatening a crushing answer.

vi

In villas, hotels, rented rooms, castles, retreats
you wrote on our bodies with your heart's racing beats:

Lou, Clara, Elizabeth, Anna, Gertrud, Elena, Ninette,
Camille, Christiane, Hedwig, Erika, Marthe, Annette,

Elsa, Loulou, Claire, Marina, Aline, Imma, Sidie –
double and treble-barrel names as you courted nobility...

You took us and left us with our grief which you said
dies into a thing. Were we anonymous in bed?

Yours the cop-out of an aesthete, no Adonis at all.
You told Lou you were no good a lover despite us in thrall.

In villas, hotels, rented rooms, castles, retreats
you cosseted Solitude, spilled your seed on fresh sheets,

visions of us more provocative to you than our skin,
though your letters insisted you preserved us within.

Your correspondence contradicted you, would not let us go –
in German verse, French prose, like journals on public show

your words dressed us in feathers, silks, satins and lace,
yet never a long lease, nor commitment could you face.

Baronesses, Princesses, Countesses, Fraus and Fräuleins;
our breath only of statues... such as Paula, Baladine.

vii

This 'house of our heart'

where we lived at your insistence,
our life together always postponed.
How you hand-wrote me into fiction,
dipping pens into ink-wells filled
with my blood. *Dear Clara, Dear*

Clara: diary entries, nature-notes,
letters, city-jottings, travel logs –
my sleeping form your hearth
a goose-wing brushed, the root
I turned into an earthenware pot.

This 'house of our heart'

day-bright from the light in stones
quarried from the maxims in your head;
quiet at night unless a vixen screamed,
for me, her mating call. Four years
a bride with only a maiden-name.

You addressed me still as 'thou', formal
as a statue on guard over my solitude
like your own at the wind-carved door,
the heather-sprigs I sent you to scent
verses: markers in your latest book.

This 'house of our heart'.

I would have chosen aprons of canvas
plaster-stiff at my plinths, bricks
and mortar, seasonal growth in gardens
through hushed intimacies of touch.
Not separate flats in Paris, rendezvous

on Sundays only, in pâtisseries –
poker-backed over galettes, black tea.
Nor would I have stooped to the role
of concierge in the basement that you
extended for fancy women map-wide:

this 'house of our heart'.

I needed your voice – not its echo –
like the music you feared unless played
in a cathedral directly to God.
Into my bronze head of you I sculpted
the tenderness, already too public,

of your love-making face, inscribed
along your hair-line my Buddhist texts.
Unread, they came out through you:
Keep desertion holy, poverty
a fullness in the house of our heart.

viii

As the skies play around you,
looping the world's loop,
dropping like stage curtains,
then lifting up, you borrow

thermals from your angels
to retrieve more than you manage
from memory so that what you receive
in your fullest being is consumed

without trace in your blood,
not a single fact in your head.
From cracks in your closed eyelids
you pull, still, endless yards

of daydreams. But, catching onto tabs,
purple, orange and grey, of ribbons
of sleep, you escape that net
tangling tighter with every effort

made to get free. And you endure
in the here and now, letting
things happen in your great gestation.
No matter if you deem women

better equipped for love, and,
in your most secret being, admit
that, like the troubadours, Dante,
you skirt merely around it,

masked in word, song, epic.
The standpoint of the angel you desire,
that workaday angel, steel-winged,
who can return to things

their laric value, then convert
for you the abstract into the concrete,
nomen into numen, furnishing
with the intimate this estranged world,

the annunciations woven
into your tone defining
their indefinableness and pointing
always just beyond the given.

As the skies play around you,
looping the world's loop,
you re-appear through stage curtains,
giving your life and death the slip.

ix

Was it nightingales your angels emulated:
calling in tremolos from a deserted garden
with their souls, glass-clear, like one soloist
exorcising a world long awaited?

Secretive, nocturnal, operatic composers,
their repertoire hinting at a beyond...
Did you feel – with their full-throated triplets
and arpeggios on speech's edge – a bond?

And let your lines improvise to their music,
teasing new theories of phrasing and motifs
from pitches outside the harmonics
of the human ear? Did you take your pick

from pipings, carols, signature tunes,
schooled in such territorial recitals
of long Latin constructions and metrics
sung, like you, from deep cover, for rivals

and each other? Lilac bushes by the orangery
felt the passion as choir-stalls of branches shook.
In the theatrical silences, you took out your book,
transposing, into ink, winged unnameable keys.

x

Your death-bed requirements: Valmont,
clean linen, night-shirts, soft white or beige
from a sales catalogue, books for the journey

to the South of France, possible now only
in your head, the straight talk of the sea,

no last sacraments, no clergy;
a nurse who does not know your poetry,
who reads to you the *Chronique Mondaine*

from *Le Figaro,* though you hated newspapers,
to append you to the trivia of the daily

which you repeatedly wrote was death
to a relationship in letters like homilies.
Nanny Wunderly in the afternoons

reciting from *Les Cahiers Verts* –
Proust, provoking remembrances,

French the last tongue in your ears –
the adopted rather than native
stressing your preference to become

invisible, alone in whatever Language
you built into a permanent home –

forbidding her to stop when she thinks you
asleep with your shout: 'Continuez!'
No medical diagnosis, sublimating

demons hidden in flowers of your anxiety.
No friends, lovers, no comforting words;

just the hand-squeeze of a doctor,
the wheeling outside of a bird
and your eyes fixed on someone near:

through shredded missives, Lou picking up
on you with her sixth sense from afar,

until you sit up, your blue eyes wide open,
stilled into those of a visionary.
And a cold wind blows over you

from across the sea that has travelled
to you, wave upon wave in a lullaby.

xi

Your angels tap-dance with the rains,
clickety-click, nothing insubstantial
about their formal steps, metal on wood.

Borrowing plumes from horses
on carousels, they sashay with trees
across horizons, choreographed

by the breeze. Waltz, tango, foxtrot,
Charleston… they know the moves
and fling off corsets lacing them

into convention. Daredevils, they swing
from beaks of crows on telegraph wires
and nose-dive to sweep out,

with splayed wings, rats from drains.
As if in Vaudeville, they stomp
on the hammers of pianos – ruining

concert pitch. Though they knock out
guardian angels, they give a singing
to the unheard that surpasses the heard,

to the ragtime movements in stillness.
Migrating flocks scatter at their approach.
Not many go near them.

xii

Dottor Serafico, no wonder earth froze.
Grave-diggers battled with the thud
of clods that would not melt as you chose

deliberately the new year's cusp
on which to attempt to die, knowing
how ghosts then stalk the living

and in shades make clouds of their breath.
Nothing new – your life always full of death.

Serafico carissimo, a Catholic by birth,
did you revert to the little mountain church
for stone angels on tombs to borrow mirth

from your angels? And dance with children
whose frozen-blue fingers held up your wreaths?
For you, there was always above and beneath

no ground-level for the horses and sleigh
bearing your coffin to slide along. Only a way

for the harness bells' jingle, the mercury
of the Rhône to carry you on and on over peaks,
in formation with birds, snaking through valleys

where woods genuflected to the Angelus.
As the children sang, you gave back the wreaths
for the deaths they would carry through life,

then dug up your own. Serafico carissimo.
Organ and violin play Bach with accelerando

for you still, settling you in the house designed
by Rodin on the site of himself: a refuge over which
he is the sky that he numbered and signed;

he is the forest and stream from a world
without hunger, separateness or desire, where one
has no self, no boundaries. Just a carillon.

Beyond Raron, Dottor Serafico, Serafico Dottor,
our sight now is insight. No asking for more.

Lost footsteps

La Salle des Pas Perdus

Camille speaks

In the corner of the room, beneath the recitative
of cackles from the female inmates in third class,
the pianola rescued from scrap creaks out its tunes.

Its felt-covered fingers have no agility, no talent
for rubato, dynamics or pedalling, as they push up
through perforated holes in rolls of cardboard sheets.

I sit in another corner, listening to the rip and tear
of minds like thick sheets, the *salle des pas perdus* a hole
where the segregated, clad in folds of emaciated skin,

Clotho-like, leap sideways. Their clumsy arabesques –
unrelated to art nouveau, to the intricacies of Islam –
mock Debussy's *Arabesque No 1* with its cascades

of triplets that, despite the heavy mechanics, waterfall
through me. No one knows I was his lover, my right hand
in my left as if it were in his; how I re-shape the women

into the fluent curves of showgirls in the Folies Bergère
until they grace his music, lips reddened by cherry-juice,
cheeks rouged by cochineal stolen from bottles

reserved for dyeing the icing on cakes of the first class.
Yet when their empty charcoaled eyes and open legs lift up
for soldiers who come to steal, from the walled gardens,

vegetables we have home-grown, they trip over
their hanging skins, flailing back through my sight, through
the notes missed or misplayed, mad for the feel of any man.

Over and over the *Arabesque* repeats, and into it I inject
the expression recorded in my heart he called too hard for his.
What the tone-deaf women register I relegate to the backs

of monkeys on hurdy-gurdy barrels once drawn
by horses to the fairground of my young life, before
its slow burial in the sound-box of *la salle des pas perdus*.

Occupation

for the Resistance leaders/poets who hid out in the area around the asylum

While enemies patrol the corridors,
clanging chains, kicking in doors,
rations of more than food, I join forces
in spirit with René Char, Aragon
under *La Danse Macabre* of Saint-Saëns.

I see their shadows stealing over walls,
stretching across lawns when day stalls.
I offer them the disguise of my dark shape.
My every breath fans the flames
of their plots against presences that maim.

In my own war-zone I am partisan
with the lopings of René Char, Aragon.
My feet tap to the percussion
of explosives powdered from paranoia.
Named here by a class and number,

I need no pseudonym to resist the figures,
white-coated, who shoot – from apertures
in my 'sanity', into the skies they drug –
my 'delusions', then drop from parachutes
the Milices' studded, polished boots.

I honour them: René Char, Aragon –
their signatures scrawled by slugs on stone,
ghosts of themselves as they slip
into dug-outs of their own sharp minds
whose underminings twist and wind

through codes they write on lavender lines.
On summit rocks I can read their signs.
I march up and down my room
in the small, sleepless hours with no radio:
only a bat's high frequencies. I cannot go

with them on backs of lorries where
they hide under scrap-iron; I cannot share
their change of skins. Yet my blood and tea
I mix for them into forging inks, save
my ammunition of endurance to stash in caves.

While gods and fates rage at odds in my head,
my feathers for flight remain under my bed.
Spa water contaminated by their *Ach, Ach, Achs*
I spit out. With René Char, Aragon
I move to *La Danse Macabre* of Saint-Saëns.

Fourteen visits in thirty years

Amer, amer regret de l'avoir abandonnée.
            Paul Claudel

Fourteen visits in thirty years
from château to asylum, from around
the world, he found her waiting still,

shrunken, dessicated, her expression
wiped clean of all anger, hostility.
She welcomed him from the iron frame

of her bed as if he appeared daily
with his similar proclivities.
Mon p'tit Paul, mon p'tit Paul.

As in childhood she muttered his name
like a song. Too late to straighten
her life-force like the pillows, too late

to reply to *Mon p'tit Paul* – as if
they were still the pair racing the woods
that ran with them, parting ears of corn.

Each time her eyes flickered open,
then shut, intense as ever, like his, he saw
what he had for so long tried to ignore:

the stations of the cross, all fourteen,
shouldered by her in isolation from her kind.
While the nurses gathered around,

blessing her new benignity,
her compliant starched simplicity,
he put his head in her hands, shock-cold.

He would nail himself to her cross.
Fourteen visits in thirty years.
Mon p'tit Paul, p'tit Paul, p'tit Paul.

Fag-ends

Camille on her Deathbed in the Asylum

i

The rusted mesh of the wireless
behind which we have all been shut
is pressing down over my face,

concentrating what is left
of me into tiny squares as my life
runs back, back, upside down,

inside out, outside in. Fag-ends
of days that have no future
struggle to delay themselves

in a present accustomed to vanishing
upon arrival, like the ghosts
in white coats, bodiless, always bodiless,

around me. On walls the plaster
flakes into figures I could have modelled:
sages, magi, jeering clowns

and jugglers that throw into the air
the stones of my last thirty years.
These, shaped by the friction of water

and cloth, I have scrubbed
my clothes with, nothing creative.
Back, back I go, over arrows chalked

in the ground by my sculptures
that run now on rickety, splint-held legs,
to the Neolithic rocks in *la grotte*

du Geyn from my childhood.
Their monstrous forms, ogre-faces,
their black lake that drowned the sun,

their giant trees that tore up the sky,
their witches that hid their own nightmares
in this nightmare territory

pre-empted where I would inhabit,
bred my demons to counteract a world
of commandments and sin, no fairytale.

100

I summon them: the Percherons of my childhood,
chains clanking as they pull load after load
of bricks from quarries into cellars in Villeneuve.

In a frieze as if along a temple wall, they stamp –
sculpted from red clay by my Tardenois region
into an eternity of labour, a percussive rhythm

in their iron shoes, feathered heels longing
for slippery grass. Carrying my brother and I
like circus riders on their dappled backs, they paw

the ground for dust to coat them in its cast.
In stalls too narrow for them to turn in, I bed them down
on straw, let them nuzzle my pockets for sugar.

Coaxing them to their feet, I undo the ropes
tying them to corroded rings, and measure what fate
has handed me out by their withers: four inches

to every hand. Between their hind legs, they lather,
not fit enough for the work I give them now: to plough
the stilled air in lines straighter than horizons

to where I have sat out my existence like a flag angled
at their vision, in the centre of boundary hedges
between sanity and insanity. While I hang onto

their straggling manes, they bolt from terracotta casts,
from the intaglio on temples, to breathe very gently through
their own steam over me. No sugar have I left to give them.

iii

*… cette terre tardenois avec laquelle elle entretient
une relation presque humaine.*
                    Camille et Paul: Dominique Bona

There he is: my father, *le chêne de Villeneuve,*
holding up the leaves of every tree,
the fixed stave around which I chanted
in the wrong order lists of all the places we moved to:

Bar-le-Duc, Nogent-sur-Seine, Villers-Cotterets,
Fère-en-Tardenois, cantons with storms, fogs,
forests, valleys, sheep and huge open fields
whose soil I fondled in my hands like a lover.

How I worked in secret, black-shawled as a peasant,
pulling up the *belles dames* – tall, elegant,
from in between endless squat *betterave* rows,
learning to sculpt a lady into clay from a weed.

And the bells. *Les cloches de L'Annonce,*
Cloches de l'Ôtage, cloches d'église, cloches
du paquebot, their ringers the swallows and swifts
that tweaked chords lighter than silk to obsess me.

Such carillons resonating through stone
I have superimposed here over the gongs
of domination clanging from belltowers, insistent
on regular scourge-sticks for the space of a *Miserere.*

They peal still in my weakening voice,
in my forsaken works – those distant now tarnished bells
in need of re-silvering by the current of the Ourcq.
Its tow-path I travel on a pack-horse of memory

to see him again, *le chêne de Villeneuve –*
waiting for me down *Le Sentier des Ocres* sculpted
by the wind, that old tutor – in defiance of those who
judged as '*un affreux malheur*' *une vocation artistique.*

iv

From my quandaries I mumble daftly to you,
my father, as if to a rosary, insisting on you
hearing my call. I probe the morning
for your nightlight to be left on.

Fingering my words barbarically,
I confide in you the way I could not
when, shut off from you behind that mesh,
I never intended to divert from the daughter

who should have progressed from birth,
baptism, communion, confirmation certificates.
Presuming now that you preferred –
to my imposed silence – the unpredictabilities

I messed over your heart, I see you wink.
And I open out for you all my stories:
the double-page spreads, the small print,
my motives, fantasies, recriminations, guilts,

half-thoughts even. On nothing do I stint
to make up for my omissions when you lived.
You edit this belly-full punctiliously, meeting
the deadline of each second that I set.

Your huge perspective makes sense of my chaos
and, as if it were my own conclusion,
I speak aloud your final comment, taking
credit for a lived wisdom not my own.

Sometimes I give you voices: of the sea, wind
or of silence itself, and I wait for you
to grace me with a syllable. Other times,
I get you to communicate by feeling.

You shiver down my spine or in a fingertip
as I test you rigorously. I intend
no emotional blackmail by constructing
my confessions into exact replicas

of the home-made night prayers whispered
by us together around my childhood bedside –
before the curtains were drawn. I have no means
of ascertaining whether the answers are yours

or those I have amended to my liking.
But, behind the mesh imposed on us
by my enemies, your moneybox tinkles still
for me. And I find in the sky a clearing.

                    v

A wireless, in my head maybe, is transmitting
a muffled performance of *La Mer*. Its sounds
squirl into shapes I can see: under-water caverns,

tidal scapes spitting over bladderwrack.
The sculptures I hacked and buried, turned into
bits of spray, stick like survivors with lichen

against the white cliffs that can be walked through
to the heart's wrecks, seaweed-smothered.
The moods change, the pictures reinforce, then

slacken the undertow, swap the pounding rhythm
for a faint timpani, just discernible in my wrist
as I struggle to push tributaries of my black veins

to their source in a perilous unconscious sea.
The reception crackles into fathoms, green, glaucous.
On their surface float bloated sailors and ferrymen

face-down, their dead eyes fixed on some Atlantis
that shifts off bedrock to spin upwards with fish.
My promised city at last with squares and fountains?

A Paris with palaces where nothing ever went wrong?
I peer down through the eyes of the drowned. Transparent
as their bodies, the sea suddenly churns and churns –

constructing designs for ancient architects to assess:
grid and radial systems – before it runs out
of itself, imprisoning me in Montdevergues' ground-plan.

vi

Chorus of Jessie Lipscomb, Henriette Thierry, Lucile – Camille's sister,
Gwen John, Rose Beuret, Clara Westhoff, Ursula Tyrwhitt, Maud Gonne

In the corridor along which you walked –
up down, down up, the duple rhythm
of your steps never changing, we button up

clown costumes and pussyfoot into your room.
Flowers cover the helplessness in our hands
as, ignoring death's neck-and-neck race,

we initiate well-tested tricks, ramming you
into our routines, with stories for you to grip,
grapes for juggling and surprises in a lucky dip.

But even the smile you assume can't keep you
familiar as, motionless, you back from days that neither
beguile nor redeem, your body a foreign precipice

your voice grows over like grass. Why, why,
we ask, should your life get away with its offence
against you and, from scrap, our hope

invent a false image of your resigned face?
We wish to apologise for our hoax of light,
our remoteness and our acts, be close enough

to say your legend will never end in our hearts.
Death is a bad private joke we can't understand,
and, like clockwork mice, we leave dumbfounded

by evasion, while you evaporate into linen
with a grace. Your eyes, defiantly matching skies,
stare from your crock that won't wind up,

throwing light back to startle animosities
into fellowship. You don't see us slump into
an early autumn that disappoints the trees,

rebuking your forsaken gods who refuse to let us
be spare parts. Exiting from the asylum, we resume,
fooling each other with out-of-season blooms.

vii

Domine non sum dignus
Ut intres sub tectum meum

He bent over her as over an altar rail,
women in décolletée reflected still
in his lusting eyes that years before had locked
into hers like a lover's, hooded, clandestine.

He bent over her like a bough from her tree
of life, invisible, grafted onto her like a mirror,
two-way, his intensities and faults doubled
in the violet blue of her still, unblinking eyes.

He bent over her. Her body was a cathedral,
unconsecrated, its pillars curved to his prayers.
The aisle of her legs led to vaults constructed
by her ribs, the cellar at her neck a Lady chapel.

He bent over her as if part of that architecture,
re-roofing worn rafters with a mumbled penance,
confessing, between the transepts of her arms,
his negligence. In the dancing, choking smoke –

he bent over her: his form an architrave for hers.
Lines she had inspired in his plays printed themselves
on this last sculpture executed without hands:
Camille-Paul, brother-sister petrified at last as one.

Sed tantum dic verbo
Et sanabitur anima mea.

viii

Show me, my women, like a queen; go fetch
My best attires…
Antony and Cleopatra V, ii

Show me, my women, like a queen; go fetch
my best attire which is also my worst:
my loose skin hanging in folds and pleats

from this emaciated skeleton I cast in plaster
long ago. Admire its crimps and folds
set by the wax, sun-heated, I poured over it –

a tried technique – from candles
collected at Compline from nuns' holders
in the Mary Chapel, by my theft unblessed.

Stitch me into it – that I might hang on
in its swirls and swathes as, no winding sheet,
it flings me, though stationary, round

and around – wild, untried, arhythmical steps
that cannot be counted – of my life's last half.
Show me, my women, like a queen. Watch me,

neither old nor young, make myself dizzy
while, Lady of my own Waltz at last, I leap off
the dust on Debussy's piano lid

to take the floor in my mind. Forget
the long, fitted jacket that showed off
my girlish curves, the hat with the plume

trembling as I shook my thick chestnut hair
for the Maître who replaced God-the-Father
as a Terror on the tail-end of the Trinity.

Take comfort while I circle about you,
partnering all my different selves, in full view
of the doves, my white mystics, lined up

outside, flapping wings for me until I am gone –
beyond the body, the mind, the lost self,
beyond the desire for a sheltering arm.

Show me, my women, as I give you the best attire
for allaying the anxiety of being alone:
the dance performing while performed. In stone.

Epilogue

Que de femmes avant nous ont fait le même chant en ce lieu.
Paul Claudel: *La Cantate à Trois Voix*

Absent fingers in the font

The money that could have helped her out
he left to the Church for masses to be said
for her after she had gone. Epistles, gospels,

offertories fell against the dilapidated walls
of the chapel, the stones quarried from her heart.
Dominus vobiscum, the priest muttered to the wind

which, standing in for the faithful, chanted
a ghostly response: *Et cum spiritu tuo* –
blowing through statues too pious to be hers,

dimpling water like absent fingers in the font.
Sanctus… the bell tinkled thrice of its own accord
into the hiatus, raw, damp, lined with the bones

of leaves she had counted falling, one by one,
in slow motion, with the bits of her life.
He should have been there, her brother,

supplicant in a pew, her name with the Virgin Mary's
on his lips, chasing away the feral cats that slinked
up the aisle, rubbing against memories of her

more recent than his, their purr prolonging
the last note of the organ now defunct.
The money that could have helped her out

rattled in the collection box, worthless as tin
without his care for her body shunted from
carré number 10 in the graveyard in Montfavet

off sacred ground to the communal ditch for the insane.
Ite missa est. The cleric's dismissal brought
no thanks to God for the way she had been flung,

anonymous, sacrificial as the bread and wine
in the mass, sealed in the earth by a line
that stretched into a tight, sadistic, spade-etched grin.